Janet Adams

PRACTICAL TOPICS FOR THE EARLY YEARS

Published by:
"TOPICAL RESOURCES"

Acknowledgements

For permission to reprint Copyright material the Editor is indebted to:

The Pre-School Playgroup Association for "There's a wise old owl" from *More Word Play & Finger Play*.

Also, for, "Five Little Speckled Frogs" from *Word Play, Finger Play*.

The Bath & District Pre-School Playgroup Association for "Clap, clap hands 1,2,3", "I can tie my shoe lace, I can brush my hair", and "John had great big waterproof boots on", from *40 Action Songs, 40 Finger Plays*.

Usborne Publishing Ltd, for "If you're happy and you know it clap your hands" from *The Usborne Children's Songbook*.

Mrs G Moore of Worksop, Notts for her poem "Softly, Softly" from *This Little Puffin* by Elizabeth Matterson published by Puffin.

Puffin Books for 22 poems from *This Little Puffin* compiled by Elizabeth Matterson Copyright © 1969.

Every effort has been made to trace the owners of copyright but we take this opportunity of tendering apologies to any owners whose rights have been unwittingly infringed.

Copyright © 1992 Janet Adams

Illustrated by Paul Sealey

Printed in Great Britain for "Topical Resources", publishers of Educational Materials, P.O. Box 329, Fulwood, PRESTON, PR2 4SF (Telephone 0772 863158) by T Snape & Company Limited, Boltons Court, PRESTON, Lancashire.

Typeset by White Cross Network, White Cross, Lancaster.

First published September 1992.

ISBN 1 - 872977 - 05 - 7

CONTENTS

COLOUR

Red 7
Red 9
Yellow 11
Yellow 13
Green 15
Green 15
Blue 19
Blue 21
All Colours 23
All Colours 25

OPPOSITES

Happy & Sad 53
Up & Down 55
Long & Short 57
Wet & Dry 59
Black & White 61
Heavy & Light 63
Big & Little 65
Fast & Slow 67
Float & Sink 69
Night & Day 71

WEATHER AND THE SEASONS

Weather Recording 31
Rain 33
Snow 35
Wind 37
Sunshine 39
Spring 41
Summer 43
Autumn 45
Winter 47
All Weathers 49

OURSELVES

My Face 75
My Body 77
My Feet 79
Lacing My Shoes 81
A Pair of Slippers 83
Hands 85
Gloves & Mittens 87
Hand Experiments 89
My Clothes 91
Counting Clothes 93

All the suggestions included in this booklet have been used in a playgroup.

Some of the illustrations can be photocopied but others will need to be enlarged.

When doing any of these activities it is important that the children are enouraged to talk about what they are doing. They will probably be able to think of songs and rhymes which illustrate each concept explored.

COLOUR

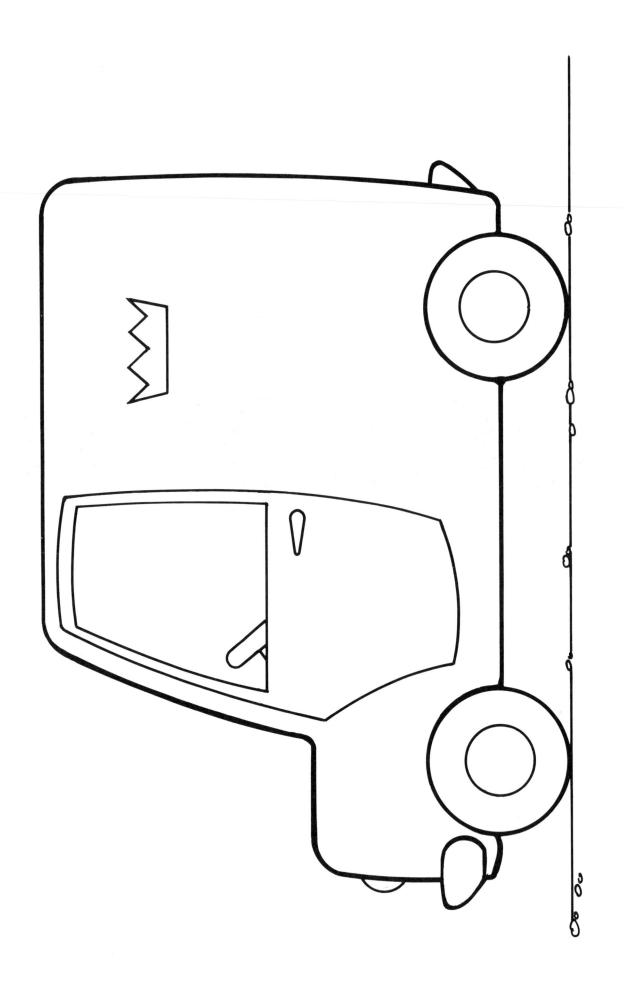

© Topical Resources. May be photocopied for classroom/playgroup use only.

RED

Make: **A Mail Van**
Painting paper
red and black paint
P.V.A. glue
silver paper/milk bottle tops

1. Either copy the van as shown opposite or make enlarged copies.

2. Paint or print with sponges the van red and the tyres black.

3. Glue on circles of silver paper or milk bottle tops as hub caps.

Listen to appropriate songs and stories.

Rhyme: One red engine chugging down the track
One red engine chugging back.

Two red engines ....etc.

Activity: Start a ' Colour and Count Book '. (see page 26)

On page one - 1 red apple (see page 27 for suitable illustrations).

Talk About: Things which are red eg. STOP sign and other road signs; letter box, fire engine, etc. Why do you think they are red?

Things which we wear/use, which are red eg. wellingtons, raincoat, shoes etc.

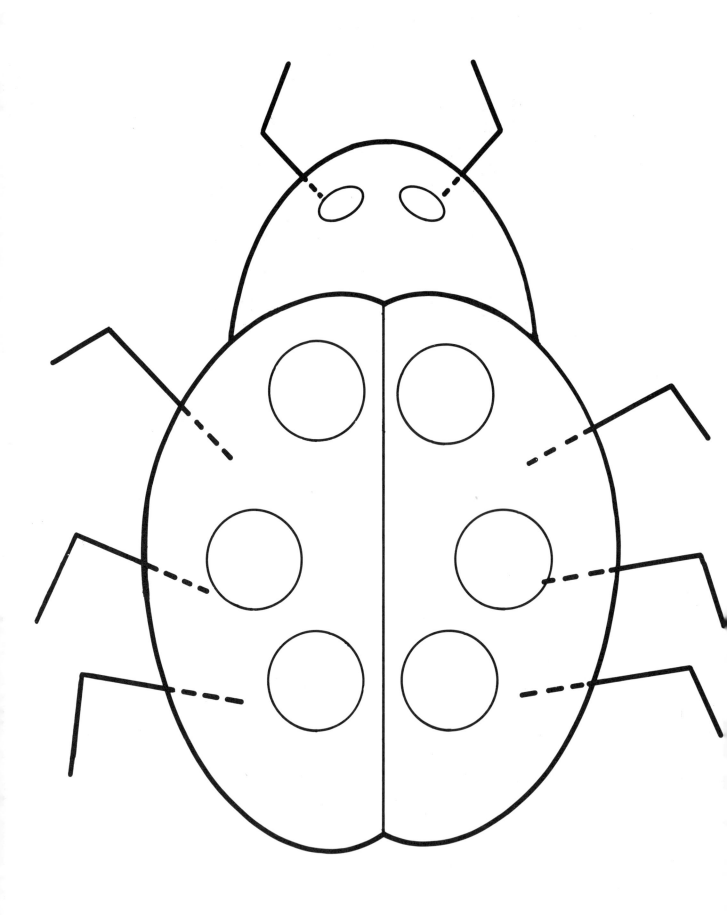

© Topical Resources. May be photocopied for classroom/playgroup use only.

RED

Make: **A Ladybird**

Red paper
Black paper
P.V.A. glue
Plastic/paper covered bag ties
Adhesive tape
White crayon/chalk
Black crayon

1. Cut out the body shape from the red paper.
2. Cut out the head shape and the spots from the black paper and stick onto the body.
3. Using the white crayon draw 2 eyes.
4. Using the black crayon draw a line down the centre of the body shape.
5. Fix bag ties with the sticky tape as shown - 6 on the body and 2 and on the head.

The ladybird can be left as it is or displayed on a leaf cut from a large sheet of green paper.

Rhyme: Ladybird, ladybird fly away home
Your house is on fire and your children all gone.
All except one and that's little Ann
And she crept under the frying pan!
                                                (Traditional)

Activity: Using a fairly flat smooth stone (from the beach), with P.V.A. glue added to the paint, paint a head black and the rest red. Stick on black felt spots.

Talk About: Stories mentioning red, eg. Little Red Riding Hood, The Little Red Hen.
Encourage the children to tell the stories and to act them out.

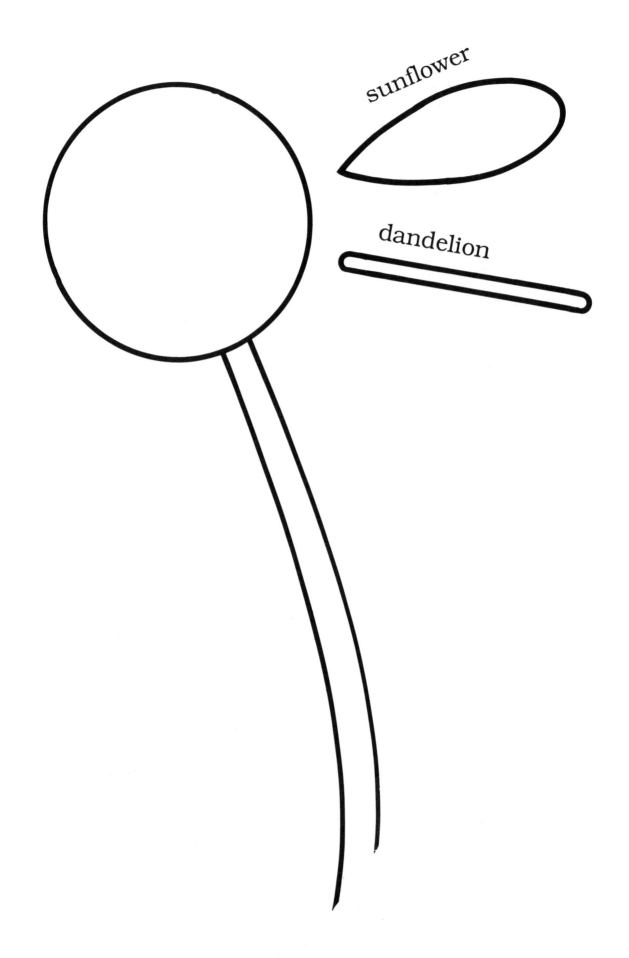

© Topical Resources. May be photocopied for classroom/playgroup use only.

YELLOW

Make: **A Flower**

Plenty of yellow strips cut from activity paper/
yellow paper from magazines
or petals from crepe paper.
P.V.A. glue
Split peas or sunflower seeds.

1. On a sheet of paper draw a circle and a stem.

2. Put glue on the circle and sprinkle on either split peas or sunflower seeds.

3. Around the circle from the back stick either yellow strips for a dandelion or petals for a sunflower.

Rhyme: **The Sunflower**

You start your life as a tiny seed
Round and green and small.
You grow so high to reach the sky,
Yellow, straight and tall.

J.A.

Activity: Page 2 for the ' Colour and Count Book'.
- 2 yellow bananas. (see page 27)

Talk About: Things that are yellow, eg. lemon, banana, sun, buttercups, chicks.

Clothes we are wearing which are yellow.

Is yellow a bright colour?

© Topical Resources. May be photocopied for classroom/playgroup use only.

YELLOW

Make: **5 Little Ducks**

Yellow activity paper or white paper and yellow crayons
P.V.A. glue
Blue paper or white paper and blue tissue paper.

1. Either fold yellow paper so that 5 ducks can be cut out at once
   or photocopy/trace a sheet with 5 ducks on it for each child to colour and cut out.

2. Either cut out a pond shape from the blue paper
   or cut out of white paper and screw up blue tissue paper and stick it on the pond.

3. Stick the five little ducks onto the pond.

Rhyme: 5 little ducks went swimming one day,
Over the pond and far away.
Mother Duck said ' Quack, quack, quack, quack!'
And only 4 little ducks came back.

4 little ducks...etc.

Activity: Use two sizes of cardboard tube, eg. toilet roll and film roll.
Dip into yellow paint and print two circles to make a duckling/ chick.
Draw on legs, beak and eye using felt pens or crayons.

Talk About: Find stories about ducklings and chickens, eg. The Ugly Duckling.

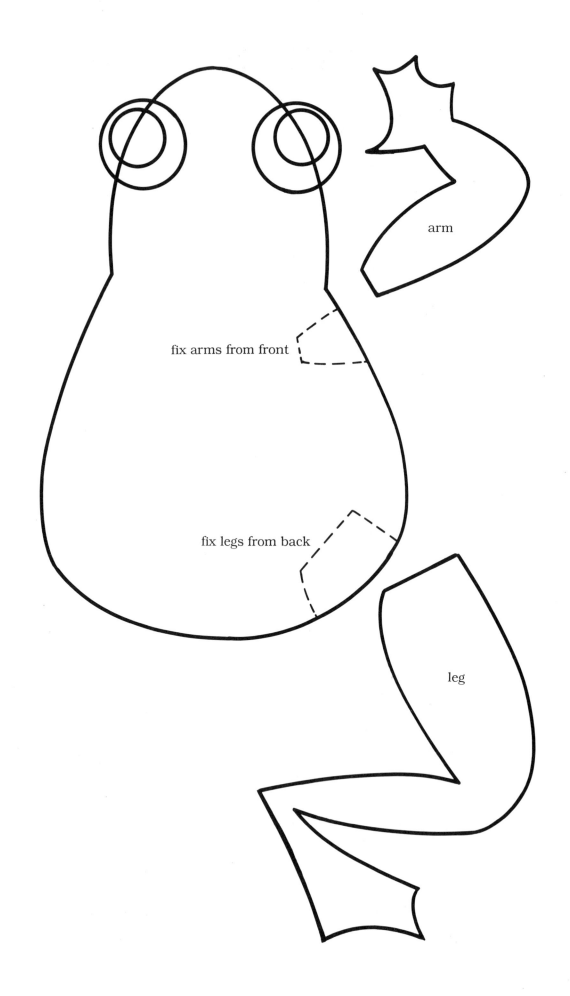

© Topical Resources. May be photocopied for classroom/playgroup use only.

Green

Make: **A Frog**

Green card
White card
Black card
Glue
Sticky tape
Fine elastic

1. Cut out the body, arms and legs from green card.

2. Cut out the eyes from the white card and the centre of the eyes from black card.

3. Glue the eyes onto the head as shown.

4. Use glue to stick the arms on at the front. Use the sticky tape to fix the legs on from the back.

5. Suspend the frog from elastic so that he can bounce.

Rhyme: 5 frogs can be made to illustrate this rhyme.

5 little speckled frogs sat on a speckled log,
Catching some most delicious bugs yum, yum!
One jumped into a pool, where it was nice and cool,
Then there were 4 green speckled frogs glug, glug!

4 little speckled frogs...etc.

Activity: Page 3 for the ' Colour and Count Book'
- 3 green pears. (see page 27)

Talk About: Insects which are green for camouflage and the reasons why.
Look for suitable pictures in magazines.

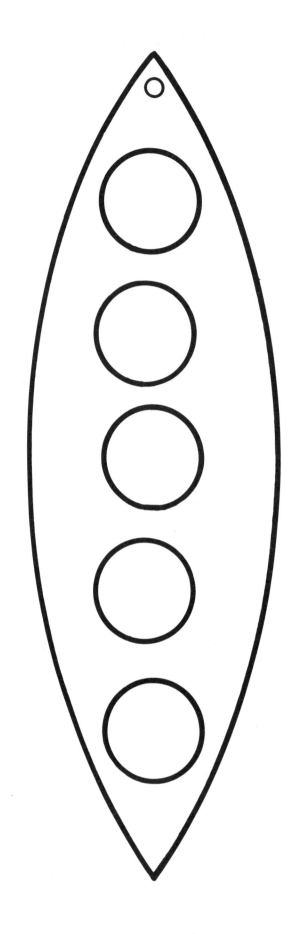

© Topical Resources. May be photocopied for classroom/playgroup use only.

Green

Make: **Peas in a Pod**

2 shades of green activity paper
Split pins
P.V.A. glue

1. Cut 2 pod shapes from one shade of green paper.

2. Cut 5 peas from the other green paper.

3. Stick the five peas onto one of the pod shades as shown.

4. Secure the second pod shape at the top of the first with a split pin so that the pod can be opened and closed.

Rhyme: 5 little peas in a pea pod pressed,
one grew, two grew and so did all the rest.
They grew and they grew and they did not stop,
until one day the pod went POP!

Activity: Find pictures of things which are green from magazines, eg. fruit and vegetables from gardening magazines and stick onto green paper.

Talk About: Things around us which are green, eg. leaves and grass; fruit and vegetables, eg. beans, peas, apples, grapes, lettuce, cress, cabbage, etc.

A display of green fruit and vegetables could be made and the children could have a taste of each.

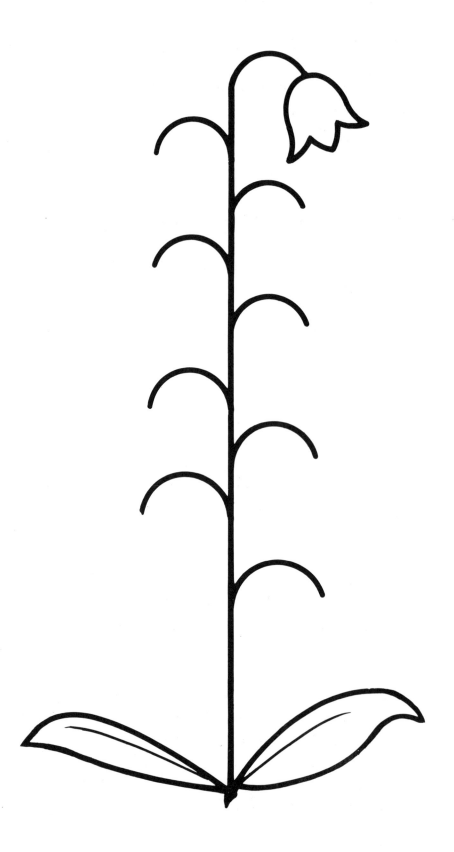

© Topical Resources.   May be photocopied for classroom/playgroup use only.

Blue

Make: **A Bluebell**

Potatoes and blue paint,
or blue and silver milk bottle tops and glue.

1. On a sheet of paper using a green pen/ crayon draw stem/stems as shown.

2. Carve out a bluebell shape in the potato using a small knife - this must never be done by the children and should be prepared in advance.

3. Use the potato to print bells onto the stem dip into the blue paint.

4. Alternatively shape the milk bottle tops into cups and stick with P.V.A. glue onto the stem.

Rhyme: (To dance around to)

In and out the dusty bluebells,
In and out the dusty bluebells,
In and out the dusty bluebells,
Won't you be my master?
(Traditional)

Activity: Although not strictly blue - 4 grapes for the ' Colour and Count Book' (see page 27)
If this is not appropiate ask the children to experiment with the blue paint by adding another colour until the colour of the grapes is achieved.

Talk About: Nursery rhymes and stories mentioning blue to act and tell, eg. Little Betty Blue, Little Boy Blue.

Blue

Make: **A Boat on the Sea**

Shades of blue paper or blue paper from magazines
Glue

1. Onto a blue sheet of paper stick on 3 layers of waves - these can be easily done if each strip of paper is folded with a wave drawn on it. Cut through the layers and open out.

2. Cut out a boat shape from another shade of blue and stick onto the picture, behind the waves as shown.

3. Draw a mast on the boat, cut out 2 blue triangles to make the sails and stick onto the picture.

Rhyme: I love to row in my big blue boat,
My big blue boat, my big blue boat.
I love to row in my big blue boat
Out in the deep blue sea.

Activity: For a quick effective way of painting sea, dip lengths of string into blue paint.
Place the dipped string onto one half of a piece of paper leaving one end of the string off the paper.
Fold the piece of paper over the string.
Move the string about inside the folded paper, then pull the string out.

Talk About: Things which are blue, eg. sky and sea, but do they always look blue?

Things in the room which are blue, are we wearing anything blue?

© Topical Resources. May be photocopied for classroom/playgroup use only.

ALL COLOURS

Make: **Teddy and his Balloons**

Crayons
or different coloured tissue paper
Glue

1. For each child draw a teddy bear or ask them to cut out a boy/girl from a magazine to hold the balloons.

2. Draw each string with its balloons a different colour, ie. red, yellow, green and blue.

3. If the balloons are drawn in dots the child can join up the dots and can then either colour the balloons in the appropiate colour or stick on screwed up tissue paper.

Rhyme: Red balloon, green balloon,
yellow, blue and white.
Floating high up in the sky
What a lovely sight.
                        J.A.

Activity: Make a simple graph to show 'our favourite colours'.
Use coloured discs for the children to stick on. Talk about the results.

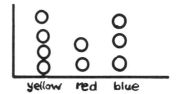

Talk About: Have a large supply of self coloured items, eg. clothes, toys, fruit, etc.
Draw circles on the floor in coloured chalks or use large hoops.
Ask the children to sort out the things and put them in the correct circles (or coloured boxes can be used).

© Topical Resources. May be photocopied for classroom/playgroup use only.

ALL COLOURS

Make: **A Butterfly**

Card or stiff paper
Paints
Thread

1. Cut out a symmetrical buttterfly shape.

2. On one half of the butterfly either drop paint onto it in blobs or paint the blobs with a brush.

3. Fold over the other half of the butterfly and press down firmly.

4. Open out carefully.

5. If the paint is very wet place another butterfly shape on the top and take off a print. When dry the butterflies can be stuck back to back down the body of the butterfly and suspended from a length of thread and displayed as a mobile.

Rhyme: I'd love to be a butterfly
With brightly coloured wings
of green and blue, pink and red
And all the joy he brings.

Activity: Cut out a simple butterfly shape.
Colour with crayons/felt pens.
Use a toilet roll tube as the
body. Put slits in the tube and
slot the butterfly onto the tube.
Large ones can be made using kitchen roll tubes.
Use pipe cleaners on the top.

Talk About: The life cycle of a butterfly and read 'The very hungry caterpillar'.

A suitable front cover for each child's 'Colour and Count Book'

For the last page draw a line of 5 circles as shown and a line of fruit. Colour the circles in the 5 different colours not corresponding with the opposite fruits. The child colours in the fruit the correct colour and draws a line to the matching coloured circle.

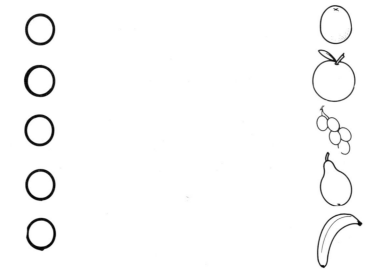

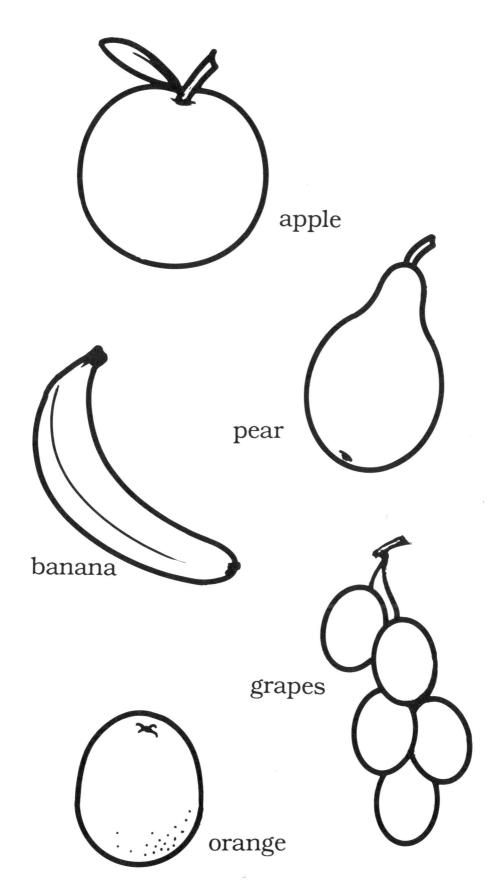

apple

pear

banana

grapes

orange

the "Colour and Count Book"
can have 5 oranges to complete it

WEATHER AND THE SEASONS

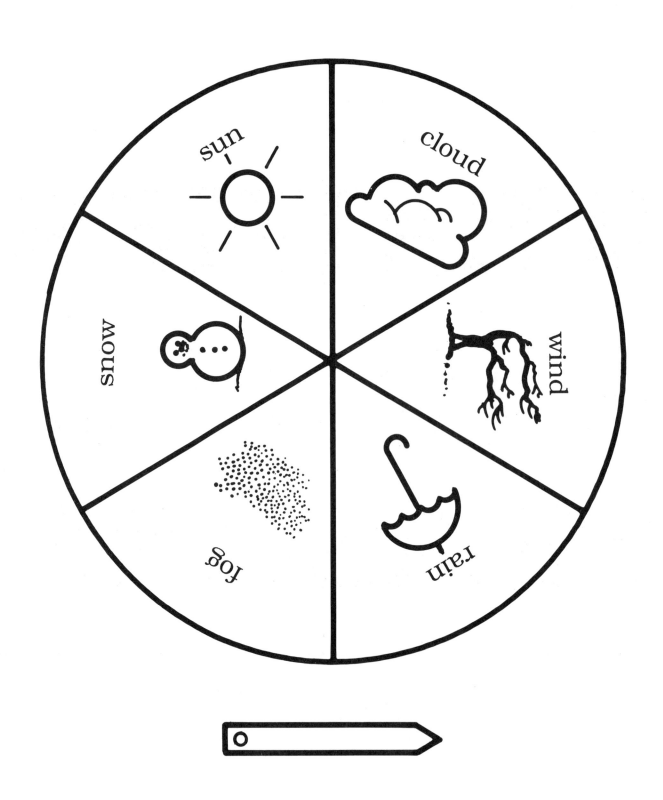

WEATHER RECORDING

Make: <u>A Weather Chart</u>

    card   split paper fasteners
    paper   glue
    pencils   crayons

The chart can be copied as shown, stuck on to a piece of card and a pointer cut from card and fixed at the centre of the chart with a paper fastener.

Or, each child could be given a circle of paper divided into 6 portions and asked to draw his own weather symbols and then colour them.
The chart should be stuck onto a piece of card to make it more rigid and then a pointer fixed at the middle, using a paper fastener.

Rhyme:

What's the weather like today?
Can we all go out to play?
We like the wind, the snow and sun,
But rainy weather's not much fun!

                                  J.A.

Activity: Cut out pictures from magazines, holiday brochures, etc., illustrating different kinds of weather. Stick the pictures onto post card size pieces of card. On a larger piece of card write 'Today it is...'. The appropiate picture can be stuck underneath.

Talk About: Look at the weather outside, what is it like today?
What is it like at different times of the year?

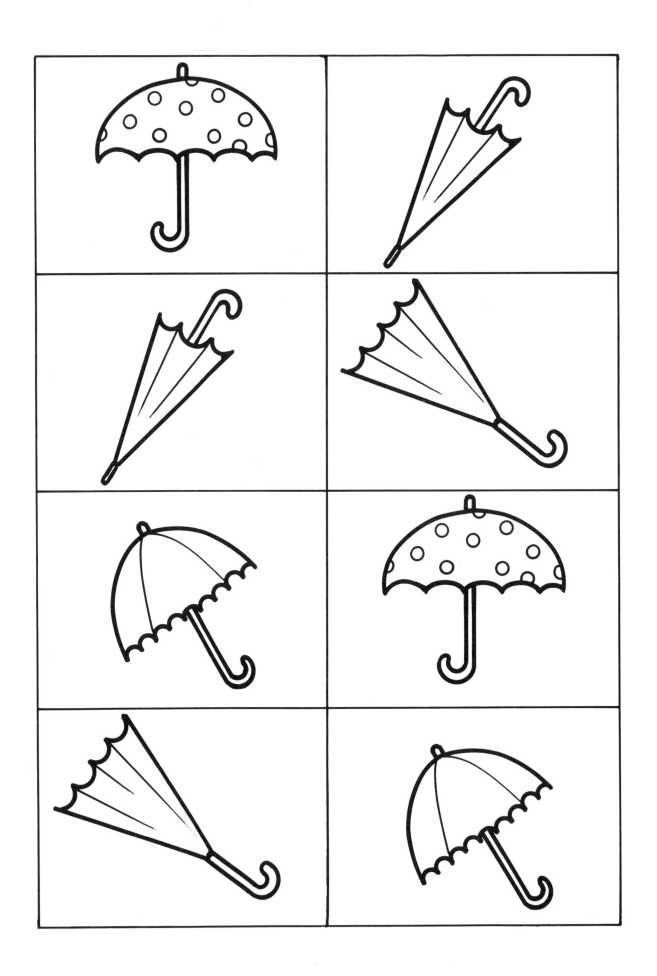

RAIN

Make: **<u>A Matching Game</u>**

        Prepared sheet
        Crayons
        Pencils

        Each child has a copy of the prepared sheet as shown.

        Match the umbrellas which are the same - the child draws a line joining up the pairs.

        Colour the matching pairs.

Rhyme: Please open your umbrella,
Please open your umbrella,
Please open your umbrella
And shield me from the rain.

        The shower's nearly over,
The shower's nearly over,
The shower's nearly over
So shut it up again.

Activity: Puddle pictures - mix a solution of icing sugar and water.
Paint the solution onto white or pale blue paper.
Whilst still wet, drop on blobs of blue ink using medicine dropper.
Watch the lovely patterns.

Talk About: Do you like the rain? What are puddles?
What happens to the countryside if it doesn't rain for a long time?
What happens if we get lots of rain?
Why do we need the rain?

If you want to make your own biscuits instead of using bought ones:

Using a food mixer
cream together: 4 oz margarine and
                    2 oz caster sugar

When light in colour add   4 oz plain flour and
                             2 oz cornflour

Bind all ingredients together.
Roll out and cut into shapes as required

Bake: 330° F for about 15 minutes.

(makes approx. 30 small biscuits).

© Topical Resources.   May be photocopied for classroom/playgroup use only.

SNOW

Make: **Peppermint Snowballs**

    1 egg white   10 oz icing sugar
    few drops of peppermint essence.

1. Whisk the egg white until frothy.

2. Add a few drops of peppermint essence.

3. Gradually stir in the sieved icing sugar.

4. Gather the mixture together in the hands to make a smooth ball.

5. The 'dough' can either be rolled out on a little icing sugar and cut with a small cutter or it can be divided between a group of children. Each child can break 'dough' into pieces and roll it in the palm of the hands to make snow balls.

6. Leave a while for outsides to harden before eating!

Rhyme: Softly, softly falling so,
This is how the snowflakes go.
Pitter, patter, pitter patter,
Pit, pit, pat.
Down go the raindrops on my hat!

Activity: Using two sizes of round, bought, plain biscuits. Place biscuits, as shown opposite onto a plate or a piece of clean, thick card. Cover the biscuits with glace icing (icing sugar and water). Stick on sweets for eyes and nose, liquorice for mouth and sweets for buttons. A hat can be cut from rice paper if wished.

Talk About: Snow, snow flakes, snowballs, snow men.
Do you like the snow?
What is like to walk in snow?

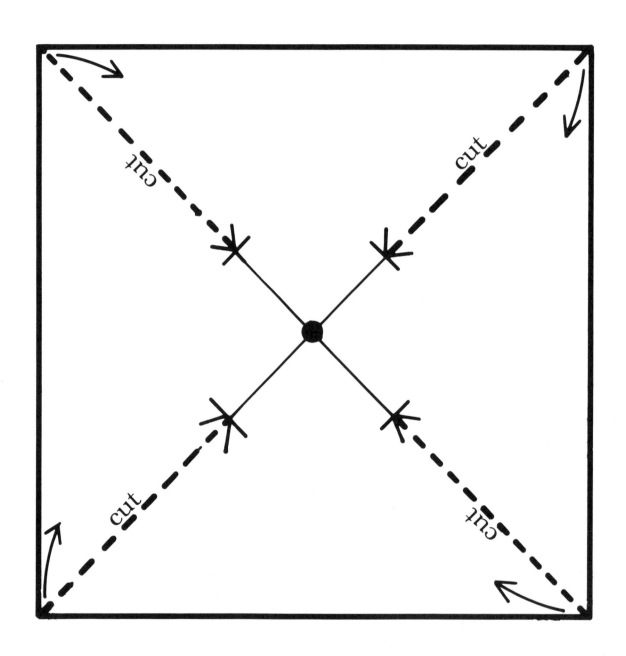

WIND

Make: **A Windmill**

coloured activity paper
drinking straws
split paper fasteners
scissors

1. Using the template opposite, cut out the shape.

2. Fold the shape from corner to corner to find the centre.

3. Cut along the folds to the marked points.

4. Bring alternate corners to the middle and fix with a paper fastener.

With adult help push the back of the fastener through a drinking straw.

Rhyme: Five little leaves so bright and gay
Were dancing about on a tree one day.
The wind came blowing through the town
OOooo ...oooo ....
One little leaf came tumbling down

Four little leaves so bright and gay, etc.

Activity: Using gummed shapes, stick triangles onto a piece of bright paper to create a kite.
Draw on a tail and add small triangles as shown.

Talk About: Have you got a kite?
Do you like going out in the wind?
How can we tell it's a windy day?
Can you see the wind?

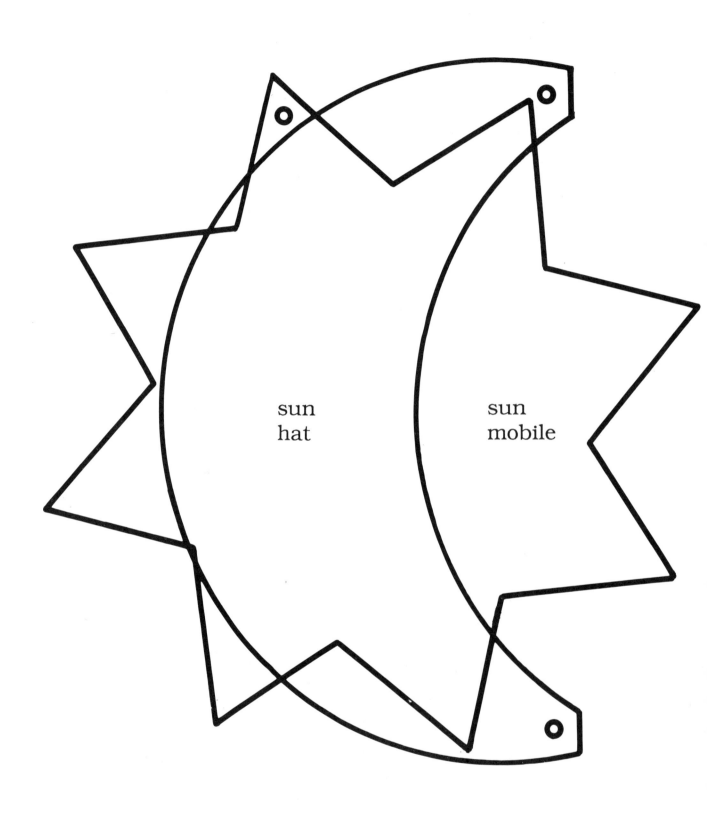

© Topical Resources. May be photocopied for classroom/playgroup use only.

SUNSHINE

Make: **<u>A Sun Mobile</u>**

Card   Glue   Cotton

Shiny paper, eg. tin foil, paper from tea/ coffee packets, chocolate wrappers, yellow cellophane.

1. Prepare templates of the sun shape as shown opposite.

2. Each child can draw round the template on a piece of white or yellow card.

3. Cut out the shape.

4. Cut out small pieces of yellow and shiny paper and stick onto the sun preferably on both sides.

5. Suspend the sun from a piece of cotton.

Rhyme: The sun has got his hat on
Hip - hip - hip - hooray!
The sun has got his hat on
And is coming out to play!

Activity: A sun hat - using the template opposite.
Cut out the shape from coloured card.
Stick on shapes cut from scraps of bright paper.
Fix on elastic according to the size of each child's head.
(The hat is worn at the front to keep the sun out of the eyes!)

Talk About: Do you like sunny days?
What games can we play on sunny days?
What would it be like if the sun didn't shine?

SPRING

Make: **Animal Masks**

    Card
    Cotton wool or animal bedding available from pet shops
    Glue
    Elastic
    Black crayon

1. Prepare mask shapes from card (old cereal packets will do)
   Each child can cut his/her own out.

2. Draw on nose and mouth.

3. Cut out the eyes.

4. Cover one side of mask with glue and stick on either cotton wool or animal bedding.

5. Allow to dry before attaching elastic.

Rhyme: Baa baa black sheep have you any wool?
Yes Sir, yes Sir, three bags full.
One for the master, one for the dame,
and one for the little boy who lives down the lane.
                                                   (Traditional)

Activity: Make a lamb from a white cotton wool ball. Glue on 2 bent black pipe cleaners for legs and colour in eyes with felt pen.

Talk About: Signs of spring, eg. buds, birds, lambs, leaves, etc.
Colours of spring.
Spring weather.

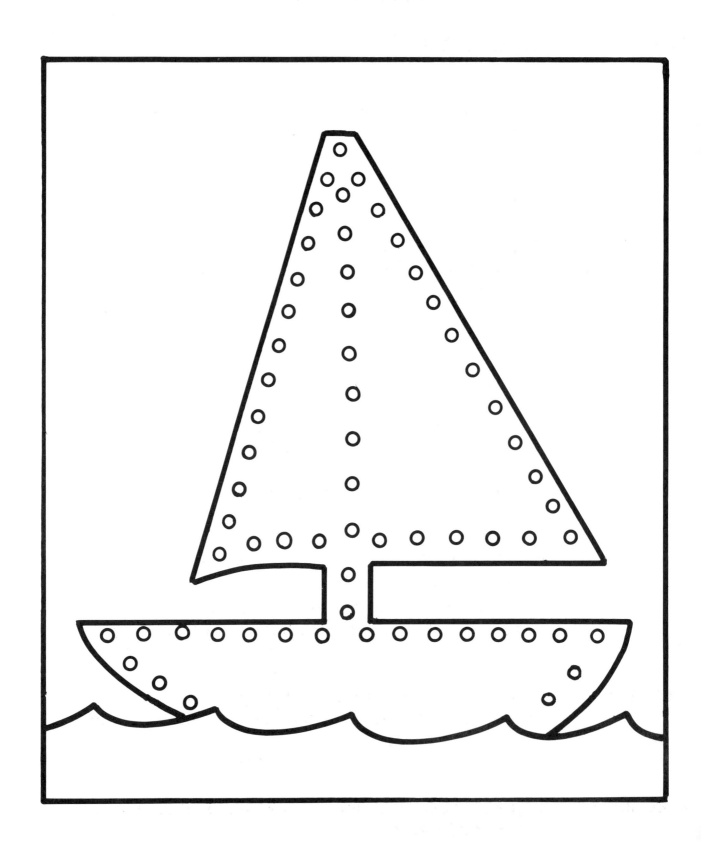

SUMMER

Make: **A Yacht**

Card
Thick wool
Blunt ended needles

Preparing your own threading cards can take a long time but if thick card is used then they can be used more than once.

1. Draw the boat as shown onto card. Cut out.

2. Punch an even number of holes in each card.

3. Tie a length of wool securely at the beginning and similarly at the end when the child has completed the card.

Let each child thread his/her own card.

Rhyme: Here is the sea, the wavy sea.
Here is the boat and here is me.
All the fishes down below
Wriggle their tails, and away they go.

Activity: Sand pictures - draw a pattern on some dark paper, using a glue stick. Sprinkle dry sand over the glue. Shake off any excess sand.

Talk About: Things we like to do in the summer.
Holidays.
Going to the beach, walking in sand, feeling it between our toes.
Paddling in the sea.
Things we can see at the seaside.

© Topical Resources. May be photocopied for classroom/playgroup use only.

AUTUMN

Make: **Matching leaves**

        Prepared sheets as shown oppsite
        Crayons
        Pencil

        Each child has a copy of the sheet shown opposite.

        He/she must colour the two matching leaves the same and then draw a line to join them together.

Rhyme:
        5 little leaves so bright and gay
        Were dancing about on a tree one day.
        The wind came blowing through the town
        And one little leaf came tumbling down.

        4 little leaves...etc.

Activity:
        Cut out large leaf shapes from brown paper.
        Let the children tear up autumnal shades from magazine pictures.
        Stick the pieces on to the leaf shapes.

Talk About:
        Walking in leaves - the noises we can hear.
        Colours of leaves in Autumn.
        Try and identify common leaves.
        Signs of Autumn.

© Topical Resources. May be photocopied for classroom/playgroup use only.

WINTER

Make: **A Robin**

Card   Black Crayon   Toilet roll tube
Red paint   Pencil   Corks
Brown paint   P.V.A glue   Scissors

1. Cut out robin using the template.

2. Colour eye with black crayon.

3. Using a cork, print the lower part of the body with red paint, and the upper part and the legs with brown paint.

4. When dry, staple or glue the robin to a quarter piece of toilet roll tube so that the robin can stand up.

The robin may be used as a serviette holder for Christmas when the tube can be covered with foil and a small piece of tinsel glued to the robin's tail.

Rhyme:

The north wind doth blow
And we shall have snow.
And what will the robin do then, poor thing?
He'll sit in a barn and keep himself warm
With his head tucked under his head, poor thing.
                                   (Traditional)

Activity: Using a round ended needle and some thick wool, thread monkey nuts and hang them outside for the birds to eat.

Talk About: Signs of winter.
What happens to the trees and flowers?
Where are the birds?
How can we look after the birds in winter?

ALL WEATHERS

Make: **A Weather Chart**

        Paper
        Pencil
        Crayons

1. Copy the sheet as shown.

2. Each child matches the weather symbols on the left with the associated objects on the right.

3. Colour the pictures.

It is important for the children to talk about what they are doing whilst they are matching.

Rhyme: Whether the weather be fine,
Or whether the weather be not.
Whether the weather be cold,
Or whether the weather be hot.
We'll weather the weather
Whatever the weather
Whether we like it or not.

Activity: In a large cardboard box have a wide selection of clothes appropiate for different kinds of weather. Let the children take it in turns to pick something out and talk about what they have chosen.

Talk About: Suitable clothes for different types of weather. If you lived in a place where it is always hot what would you wear?
If it was always cold, what would you wear?

OPPOSITES

© Topical Resources. May be photocopied for classroom/playgroup use only.

HAPPY and SAD

Make: **A Clown**

Cardboard plates   Paints/crayons   P.V.A glue
Cut out shapes for eyes, mouths and bow ties.
Coloured shredded tissue/crepe paper.

1. Crayon or paint two sets of eyes, mouths and bows.

2. Stick one set on one side of plate making it have a happy face.

3. Screw up some red tissue paper into a ball and stick on for a nose.

4. Use one cardboard plate to cut into segments making ears for several clowns.

5. Stick one pair of ears onto clown (an adult can staple them if necessary)

6. Stick on shredded paper for hair.

7. Turn plate over and make sad face.

8. Finish off by sticking on 2 bow ties, back to back.

9. Hang from a piece of threaded cotton.

Rhyme: If you're happy and you know it clap your hands,
If you're happy and you know it clap your hands,
If you're happy and you know it and you really want to show it,
If you're happy and you know it clap your hands!

Activity: On one forefinger draw a happy face and on the other a sad face. Pretend they are puppets.

Talk About: What makes us happy. What makes us sad.
Make your face happy. Make your face sad.

© Topical Resources. May be photocopied for classroom/playgroup use only.

UP and DOWN

Make: **A Jumping Kangaroo**

Card (from a cereal box will do)
P.V.A. glue with brown paint added to it.
Tights cut into small pieces.
One eye for each kangaroo from paper or card.

1. Draw round template onto card.

2. Cut it out.

3. Cover the whole of the shape with brown glue.

4. Stick on eye then drop or place the pieces of tights over the whole shape.

5. Leave to dry.

6. Suspend the kangaroo from a piece of fine elastic to make him jump.

Rhyme: Jump, jump! Kangaroo Brown.
Jump, jump! Off to town.
Jump, jump! Up hill and down.
Jump, jump! Kangaroo Brown!

Activity: A see-saw - cut out a triangle and stick onto a piece of paper.
Cut out a rectangle of proportionate size. Fix it to triangle with a brass split pin. You can stick people onto the see-saw if you wish and sing 'See saw. Margery Daw...'

Talk About: Nursery Phymes which mention ' Up and Down'.
Machines which go up and down.
Animals which jump up and down.

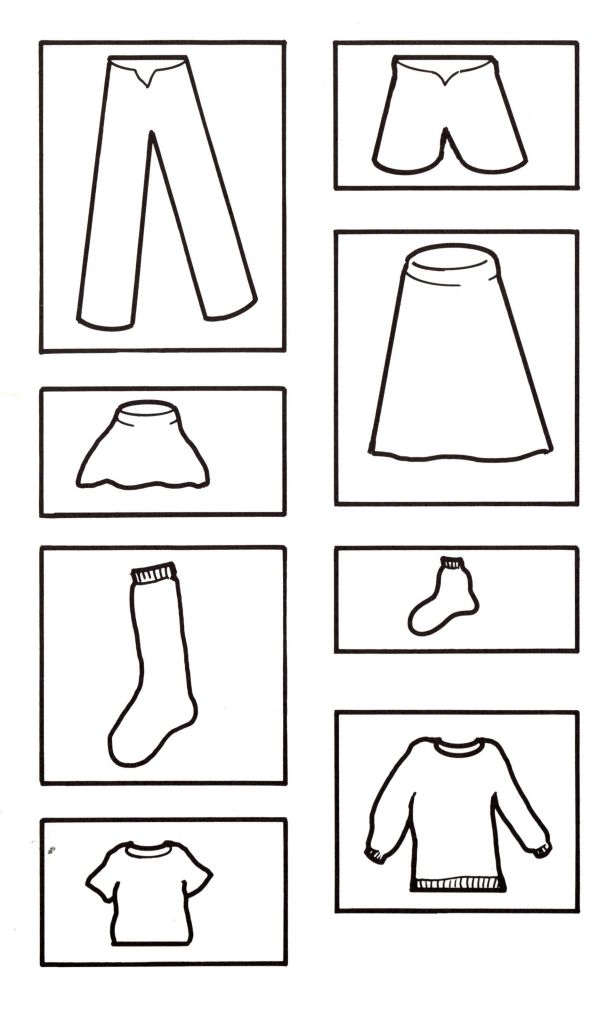

© Topical Resources. May be photocopied for classroom/playgroup use only.

LONG and SHORT

Make: **Printing Shapes**

Although this activity might take time to prepare it is one which younger children are able to do with recognisable results.

Card (laminated is most successful)
Small pieces of sponge.
Paints
Paper with a fold or line down the middle - one side for long and one for short.

1. Prepare stencils using the designs opposite.

2. Place each one in turn onto paper and sponge paint onto the shape in the middle. Carefully lift off the paper. (It is better to have quite a wide margin of card around each shape).

3. Print all the long shapes down one side of the paper and the corresponding short ones down the other side of the paper.

It is important to talk with the child whilst he/she is doing this activity.

Rhyme: An elephant goes like this and that.
He's terrible big and he's terrible fat.
He has no fingers and he has no toes.
But goodness gracious, what a nose!

Activity: Cut straws into long pieces and short pieces.
Thread onto some wool using a bodkin - a long piece, a short piece, etc. and make into a necklace.

Talk About: Who has long/short hair?
Who is wearing long/short socks, trousers, etc.
Which animals have long/short ears, teeth, feet, nose.
Make a long line of children and a short line of children.

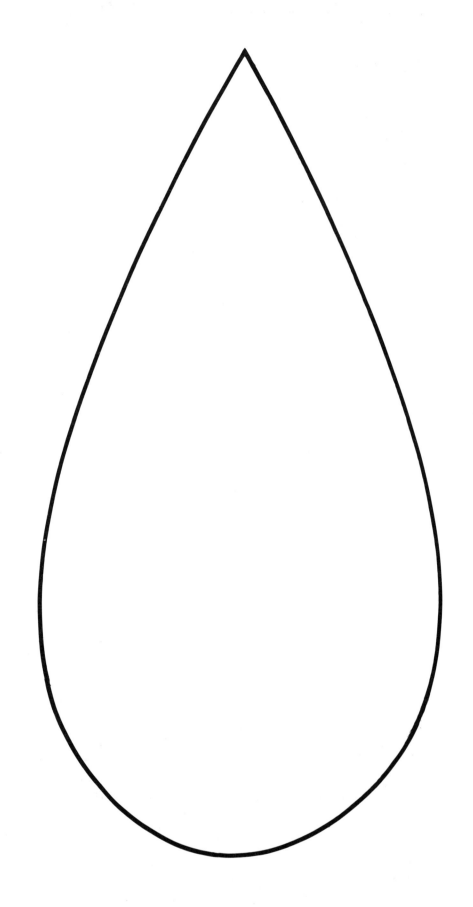

WET and DRY

Make: **Giant Raindrops**

Painting paper cut into raindrop shape
Paints
Water

1. Each child needs two pieces of paper.

2. Wet one piece of paper by painting with water using either a large paint brush or a sponge.

3. Drop different colours of paint onto the wet paper - the colours should spread out and merge together.

4. On the dry piece of paper drop different colours of paint. The effect on each piece of paper should be different.

Rhyme: I hear thunder, I hear thunder
(drum feet on the floor)
Hark don't you, hark don't you?
(pretend to listen)
Pitter patter raindrops,
(indicate rain with fingers)
Pitter patter raindrops
I'm wet through
(shake whole body vigorously)
SO ARE YOU!
(point to a neighbour)   (to the tune of 'Frere Jaques)

Activity: If there is a safe area of dry concrete outside 'paint' with water using large paint brushes.
(On a dry day of course!)

Talk About: Rhymes and songs which mention the weather.

What makes us wet, eg. rain, snow, etc. also swimming baths, shower, bath, etc.
How do we dry ourselves.
How can we keep dry.
Different clothes we wear to keep us dry.
How do we feel when we are wet/dry.

© Topical Resources. May be photocopied for classroom/playgroup use only.

BLACK and WHITE
(also Light and Dark)

Make: **Silhouettes (Shadows)**

Card   Paper   Black Paper
Crayons Glue

Prepare some templates out of card of familiar objects or shapes.
Have the same objects or shapes cut out of black paper.

1. Draw round each template in turn - one under the other.
2. Colour.
3. Find the matching silhouette and stick on the paper next to the corresponding picture.

You may find it easier for the children if the paper has been divided into sections before they start.

Rhyme: My shadow
My shadow is always with me
When I go out to play,
It follows right behind me
And will not go away.

I think when I'm asleep in bed,
My shadow sleeps as well,
I wonder if it dreams like me -
It's very hard to tell.   J.A.

Activity: Hang a white sheet over a clothes horse. Switch on a projector and shine light onto sheet. Sit children on other side of sheet. Hold up familiar objects between projector and sheet to make shadows and the children can guess what the shapes are.

Talk About: Look around for things which are black/white.
When do we see shadows?

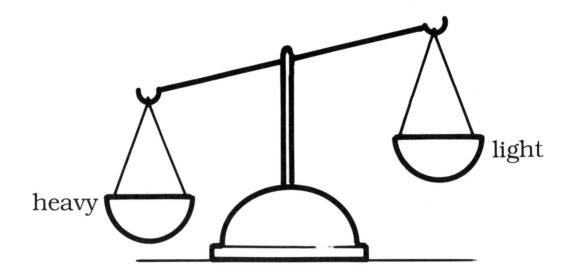

HEAVY and LIGHT

Make: <u>**A Weighing Experiment**</u>

This takes time to prepare but it will be worth it.

Choose 3 or 4 pairs of things. One of each pair - light, the other - heavy.
eg. feather and stone, empty milk bottle and plastic cup, shoe and pencil
Draw the objects on a sheet of paper for each child to colour and cut out. (Photocopied in advance)

For each child draw 2 sets of scales on a large piece of paper.

1. Organise the children so that no more than 4 at a time are involved with the weighing.
2. Choose one pair of objects. Talk about them and let the children say which they think is heavy/ light.
3. Let the children hold the objects in their hands - ask which is heavy/ light?
4. Use balancing scales to see if they are correct with their guessing.
5. To record their findings stick the appropiate pictures into the correct buckets on the scales.

Rhyme: What is light?
A kite is light.
When the wind blows
I hold on tight!
       J.A.

Activity: Cut pictures out of magazines - things which are heavy and things which are light.

Talk About: Things around us which are heavy/light.
Things that are too heavy for us to lift.
Heavy and light things at home.
Machines which are used for lifting.

© Topical Resources. May be photocopied for classroom/playgroup use only.

BIG and LITTLE

Make: <u>A Colouring Activity or Threading Activity</u>

On one sheet of paper you could draw almost anything for each child to colour.
Eg. a big and a little man, a big and a little tree, a big and a little shoe, a big and a little house, etc.
Threading is a popular activity. Cards take time to cut out and punch but the children enjoy using them.

<u>Big flower, little flower</u>
Coloured card
Thick colourful wool   Blunt ended needles

1. Give each child a large flower and a small flower. Cut out from coloured card with an even number of holes punched in each.

2. Tie the thread firmly at the start so that it won't easily become unthreaded. Similarly finish it off securely at the end.

3. Let children thread their own cards.

If you use vinyl material instead of card then the finished items can be used for a table mat and coaster!

Rhyme: about something small: Incy wincy spider,
                                            5 little peas in a pea pod pressed
                about something big: The big ship sails through
                                            the Alley, Alley - O.
                                            The wheels on the bus.

Activity: Using pre-cut gummed shapes. Fold a large piece of paper in half. One side of the fold - big, the other - little. Let the children stick on to the paper on the correct side big and little circles, big and little triangle, big and little rectangles etc.

Talk About: Look for big/little things in the room. Big and little animals. Can we make ourselves big/little?

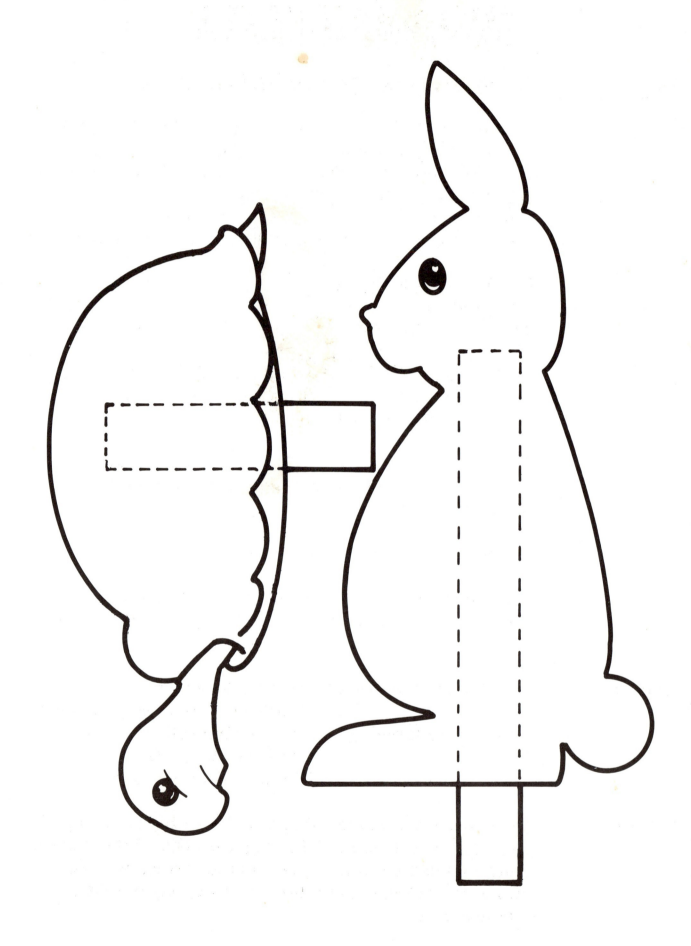

© Topical Resources. May be photocopied for classroom/playgroup use only.

FAST and SLOW

Make: **The Tortoise and the Hare Puppets**

This is an ideal story to illustrate fast and slow; also stop and go; start and finish.

Card (from cereal packets will do)   Cotton wool
2 eyes cut from card and coloured.
Shades of brown animal bedding (from pet shops)
Torn up pieces of brown paper/magazine pictures
P.V.A. glue with brown paint added.

1. Cut out the shapes and fix on a length of card onto back to support and to hold puppets by.
2. Hare - paint completely with brown glue.
3. Stick on eye.
4. Stick a blob of cotton wool onto tail.
5. Stick on brown 'fur' (need not be solid)
6. Tortoise - paint completely with brown glue
7. Stick on eye.
8. Drop brown paper bits on to the tortoise's shell.

Rhyme:
Slowly, slowly, very slowly,
Creeps the garden snail.
Slowly, slowly, very slowly,
Up the wooden rail.

Quickly, quickly, very quickly,
Runs the little mouse.
Quickly, quickly, very quickly,
Round about the house.

Activity: A toilet roll tube makes an ideal ' fast' rocket. Slot in two triangles of card. Half a small cereal box with a circle added and 4 pieces of card make a 'slow' wheelbarrow.

Talk About: Animals which are fast/slow. Vehicles that are fast/slow. When do we go fast/slow?

FLOAT and SINK

Make: **A Floating and Sinking Experiment**
This takes time to prepare!
Collect a variety of items which will float or sink. Draw them on a sheet of paper for each child to colour and cut out (photocopied in advance). Draw a tank on a large piece of paper for each child.

A glass/transparent fish tank or mixing bowl.
Crayons
Scissors
Items, eg. a plastic duck, a cotton reel, a pencil, a coin, a stone, a plastic spoon, a wooden brick, etc.

1. Fill the tank three quarters full with water.

2. Have the objects on a table for the children to see and let the children colour in the pictures of them. Cut them out and put in a safe place.

3. Have a small group of children at a time and let them take it in turns to put different objects into the water saying whether they think it will float or sink before they let go.

4. When all the objects have been tested the children have to stick the appropiate pictures onto the drawing of the tank either floating on top of the water or sinking at the bottom.

Rhyme: Any which mention boats or ships, eg. the big ship sails through the Alley, Alley, O.
Fishes and ducks, eg. 5 little ducks went swimming one day.

Activity: Using the construction toys you have available, eg. Lego, Duplo, etc. let the children make boats and test them in a sink to see if they float or sink.

Talk About: Going swimming - do we float or sink. What can we use to make us float. Different kinds of boats.

© Topical Resources. May be photocopied for classroom/playgroup use only.

NIGHT and DAY

Make: **An Owl and a Robin**

Card
Crayons
Scissors
Glue

According to the age and ability of each child the shapes can be cut out for them or by them.

1. Cut out owl and separate eyes.

2. Colour owl on both sides.

3. Colour eyes and stick onto owl.

4. Cut out bird and colour on both sides.

5. Cut out wings, colour and slot onto back.

6. Hang both birds with cotton from a small branch.

Rhyme: There's a wise old owl
With a pointed nose,
Two tufty ears and claws for toes.
He sits in a tree and looks at you,
Then he flaps his wings and says,
' Whoooo - oo!'

Activity: Use black paper, yellow and white paint - let the children paint a night time picture.
Use white paper, blue, red and green paint - paint a day time picture.

Talk About: People who work in the day time/night time.
Differences between night and day.
Animals which only come out at night time/day time.

More Opposites

fat and thin
hot and cold
deep and shallow
rough and smooth
clean and dirty
good and bad/naughty
wide and narrow
tall and small/short
old and new/young
tidy and untidy
in and out
inside and outside
open and closed/shut
under and over
on and off
front and back
empty and full
top and bottom

OURSELVES

© Topical Resources. May be photocopied for classroom/playgroup use only.

MY FACE

Make: **A Face**

Pink Card   Pink cotton wool balls
Scraps of brown, black and yellow wool
Red felt   P.V.A glue
Cut out brown, blue and green eyes from material/card

1. Cut out pink card circles for the head.

2. Stick on the appropiate colour of wool according to the colour of the child's hair. If the faces are going to be hung up like mobiles then stick wool on the back of head.

3. Stick on the appropiate coloured eyes.

4. Prepare mouths from the red felt and stick one on the face.

5. Stick on a pair of pink ears.

6. Either hang the finished face from a piece of thread or display on the wall.

Before making a face talk about the position of the eyes, ears, nose, mouth, chin. What colour is your hair? Use a mirror and ask, what colour are your eyes?

Rhyme: Two little eyes to look around,
Two little ears to hear each sound,
One little nose to smell what's sweet,
And one little mouth that likes to eat!

Activity: Used commercially produced geometric shapes to stick on a circle of paper to make different faces.

Talk About: How many eyes, ears, noses, mouths have I got? What are they used for? Curly/straight, long/short hair. How we can tell the way a person feels by looking at their face: eg. happy, sad, angry, surprised, frightened, etc.

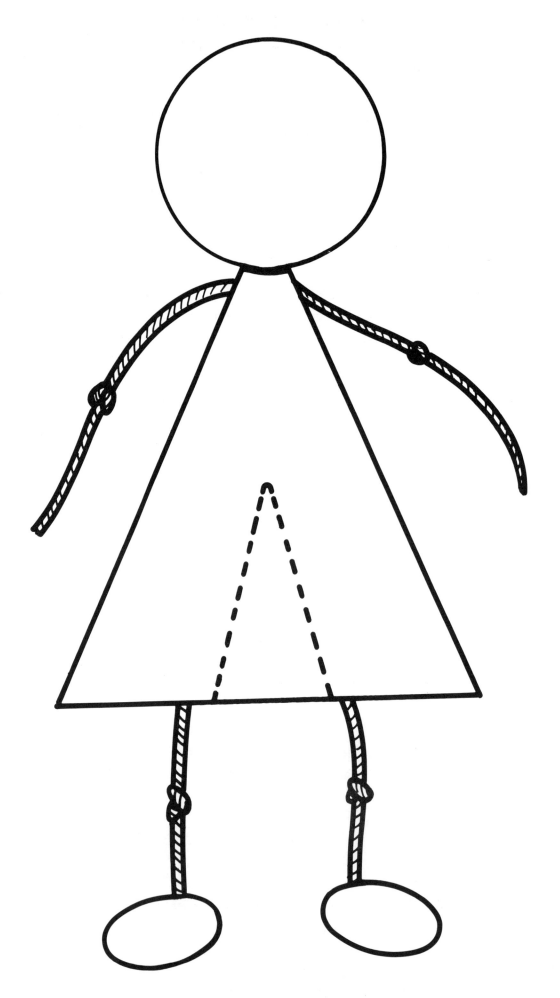

© Topical Resources. May be photocopied for classroom/playgroup use only.

MY BODY

Make: **Lanky Lucy/Lenny**

Cut out faces from catalogues or photographs
Coloured card or activity paper
String   P.V.A. glue

1. Cut out oval of paper the size of the cut out face.

2. Stick face onto paper.

3. Cut out 2 triangles for a skirt or 2 trouser shapes from the card/activity paper.

4. Cut a length of string; sandwich and glue between the two skirt/trouser pieces towards the top.

5. Knot the string halfway down the arms to make elbows

6. Cut a length of string for legs and secure near bottom of skirt/trousers.

7. Knot the string halfway down the legs to make the knees.

8. Cut 2 circles or ovals for each shoe, sandwiching and gluing the string into place.

The finished person can be hung up as a mobile or used as a puppet.

Rhyme: Head, shoulders, knees and toes, knees and toes.
Head, shoulders, knees and toes, knees and toes.
And eyes and ears and mouth and nose.
Head, shoulders, knees and toes, knees and toes.

Activity: Draw/paint a picture of ' Me'. Ask the children to bring photographs of themselves and make a display with them.

Talk About: Where are different parts of the body - eg. knees, elbows, shoulders, neck, chest, tummy, back, etc.

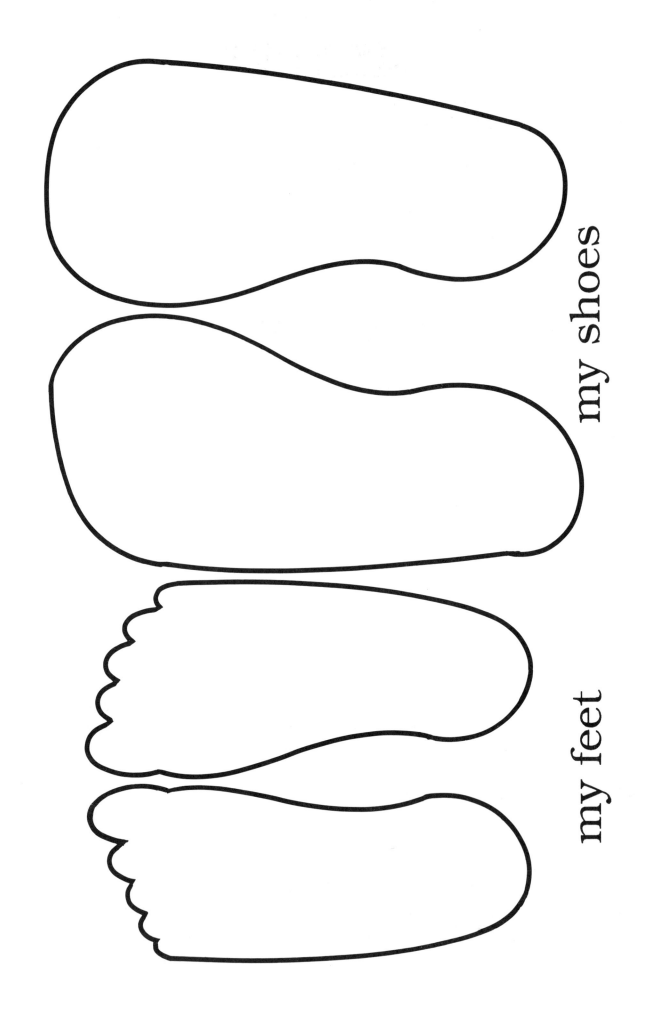

MY FEET

Make: **Feet Shapes**

Suitable size paper
Pencils
Wax crayons

1. On one piece of paper per child, draw round their bare feet, counting the toes as you do so.

2. Either an adult or the child with help, draw round their shoes.

3. Colour the shoes in the correct colour.

Rhyme: Can you walk on tip-toe as softly as a cat?
And can you stamp along the road
Stamp, stamp, just like that?
Can you take some great big strides
Just like a giant can?
Or walk along so slowly
Like a poor bent old man?

Activity: Footprints - instead of dipping the feet into a bowl of paint it is less messy and there are less drips if the children stand on a large sponge which has been dipped in paint and standing in a washing up bowl. Once the feet have paint on them let the children walk along a strip of paper (eg. use an old roll of wallpaper).

Talk About: Our feet -
 how many toes; parts of the feet,
 eg. toes, nails, ankles, heels, etc.

Different ways of moving on our feet
 eg. walking, running, jumping, stamping,
 striding, marching, on tip-toes etc.

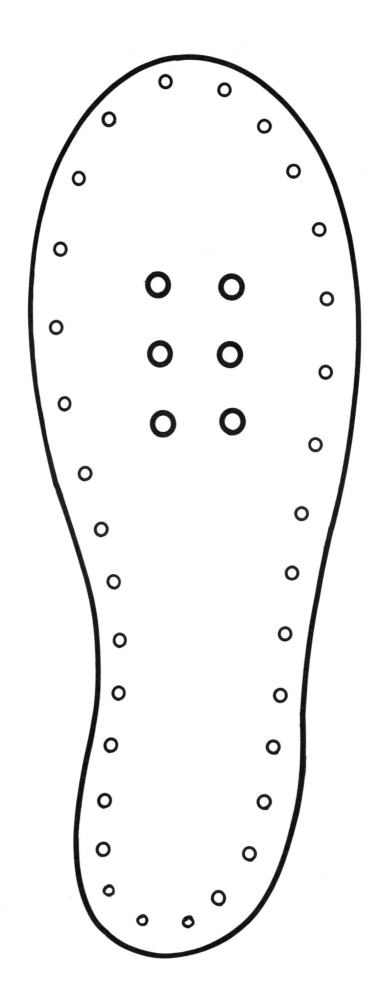

© Topical Resources. May be photocopied for classroom/playgroup use only.

LACING MY SHOES

Make: **A shoe shape to lace**

    Cut out card shoe shapes
    Blunt needles
    Wool

1. Cut out shoe shapes and punch an even number of holes in each.

2. Make 6 extra holes in the middle as shown.

3. Tie the thread firmly at the start of the outer holes and similarly finish it off securely at the end.

4. Let each child thread their own card.

5. Help will be needed to thread a length of wool for the middle holes and in tying a bow.
   This can be frequently used as a child learns how to tie his own shoe laces.

Rhyme: My wellington boots go thump - thump - thump.
    My leather shoes go pit - pat - pit.
    But my rubber sandals make no noise at all.

Activity: Have a large box containing a variety of footwear.
    The children have to pair them up and talk about them,
    eg. when might they be worn?
    Who might wear them? etc.

Talk About: Our shoes:-
- are you wearing shoes, boots, sandals, trainers, slippers?
- What colour are they?
- What sort of fasteners have they got?
- eg. velcro, buckles, laces.

Putting shoes on the correct feet - right and left.

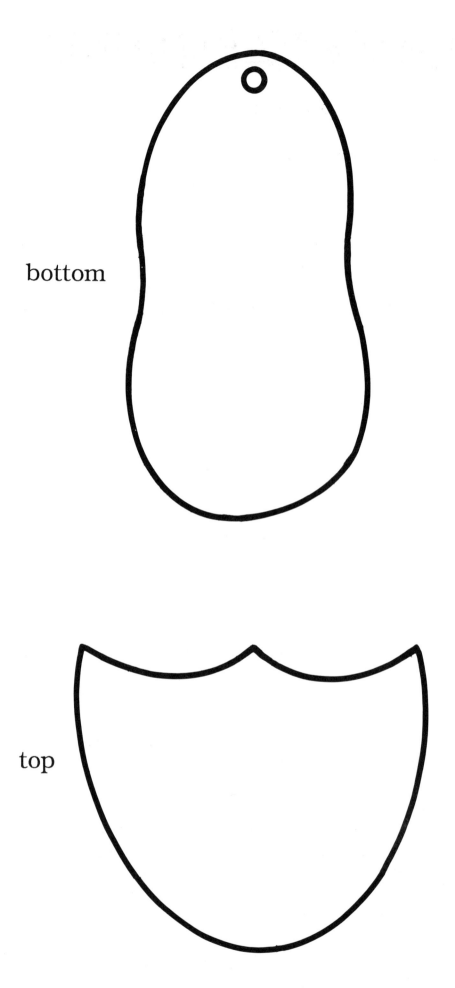

© Topical Resources. May be photocopied for classroom/playgroup use only.

A PAIR OF SLIPPERS

Make: **A Pair of Slippers**

Old birthday cards
Glue
Cotton

1. Cut out 4 shapes from old birthday cards.

2. Glue each top piece to a bottom piece along the edge - it will not lie flat but will be raised up like the front of a slipper.

3. Make up a hole at the end of each slipper and tie together with a length of cotton.

Rhyme: Diddle, diddle dumpling my son John.
Went to bed with his trousers on.
One shoe off and one shoe on,
Diddle, diddle dumpling my son John.
(Traditional)

Activity: Cut out footwear from old mail order catalogues. Stick onto a sheet of paper or make a little book 'My book of shoes'.

Talk About: Different footwear for different weather, eg. sandals, wellingtons, flip-flops, shoes.

Different footwear for different jobs.

Different footwear for different members of the family.

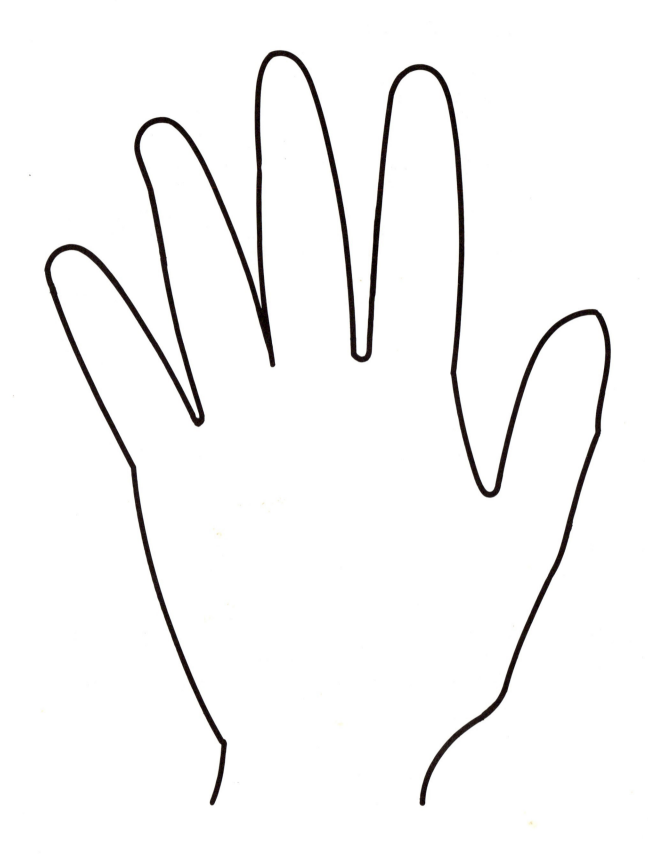

© Topical Resources. May be photocopied for classroom/playgroup use only.

HANDS

Make: **A Hand to Trace**

                Paper
Tracing paper
Pencils

1. Draw round an adults hand or copy the one illustrated and have a copy for each child.

2. Fix a piece of tracing paper over each hand with staples, glue or sticky tape.

Each child traces over the hand and can colour the underneath hand if wanted.

Rhyme: Tommy Thumb, Tommy Thumb where are you?
Here I am, here I am, how do you do?

Peter Pointer - Toby Tall - Ruby Ring - Baby Small
- Fingers all.

Activity: Painting with hands and fingers.
Drawing round each others hands.

Talk About: Parts of the hand eg. knuckles, palm, fingers, thumbs.
Counting fingers and thumbs.
Using our fingers in a number rhymes and operating puppets.

© Topical Resources. May be photocopied for classroom/playgroup use only.

GLOVES AND MITTENS

Make: **A Mitten Matching Game**

Templates of glove and mitten
Different coloured paper
Glue

1. Using the templates, cut out pairs of gloves and mittens out of coloured paper.

2. Stick one of each of 4 pairs on a sheet of paper (two pairs of gloves and two pairs of mittens)

3. Each child has to stick on the matching mitten/ glove in the correct shape/colour.

Rhyme: Point to the ceiling,
Point to the floor,
Point to the window,
Point to the door,
Clap your hands 1, 2, 3
And put your hands upon your knee.

Activity: Have a box of different gloves and mittens, let the children pair them up and peg them in their pairs on a washing line.

Talk About: The way we use our hands to mean certain things, eg. come here; bye bye; hush; stop; etc.

The way we use our hands to play musical instruments.

Actions we do with our hands

e.g.

screwing
pushing
pulling
posting
banging
dropping
throwing
rolling
} find an assortment of toys which demonstrate these skills

Fasteners

e.g.

button
zip
poppers
velcro
laces
buckle
tie
toggle
} find items of clothing which have a variety of fasteners

Touch

e.g.

rough
smooth
hard
soft
heavy
light
prickly
thick
thin
wet
} find a variety of materials which illustrate a wide range of textures and qualities

Matching

e.g.

rubber gloves
surgical gloves
oven gloves
motor cyclist's
woolly mittens
sheepskin mittens
evening gloves
gloves of different sizes for a family
} have a variety of different gloves and mittens for matching and for talking about.

HAND EXPERIMENTS

Make: **Hand Activities**

Have 4 boxes containing items for each of the 4 groups as shown opposite.

It is important that an adult is with each group to encourage the children to talk about what they are doing.

Gathering all these things together takes time but it is well worth it.

Rhyme: Clap, clap, hands 1, 2, 3
Put your hands upon your knee
Lift them high to touch the sky,
Clap, clap hands and away they fly.

Activity: Have a collection of instruments which are played with the hands, eg. drums, tambourines, triangles, bells.

Sing a nursery rhyme and accompany the singing with the instruments and clapping.

Talk About: How important our hands are to us and how difficult it is to do lots of things if we are unable to use our hands.
What do you use your hands for?
What is it like if we hurt our hands and fingers and have to wear a plaster or a bandage?

© Topical Resources. May be photocopied for classroom/playgroup use only.

MY CLOTHES

Make: **A Figure to Dress**

Prepared outlines of boys and girls
Crayons

1. Prepare outlines. One for each child.

2. Let each child colour in the clothes according to what he/she is wearing.

Rhyme:
I can tie my shoelace,
I can brush my hair,
I can wash my hands and face,
And dress myself with care.
I can clean my teeth too.
And fasten shirts and frocks.
I can say 'How do you do.'
And pull up both my socks!

Activity: Use old mail order catalogues and magazines for children to cut out 'Clothes I like to wear', and stick onto a sheet of paper or a concertina of paper to make a booklet.

Talk About: The clothes we are wearing today.
What colours are they?

Indoor and outdoor clothes.

Clothes for cold and hot weather.

Clothes for special occasions.

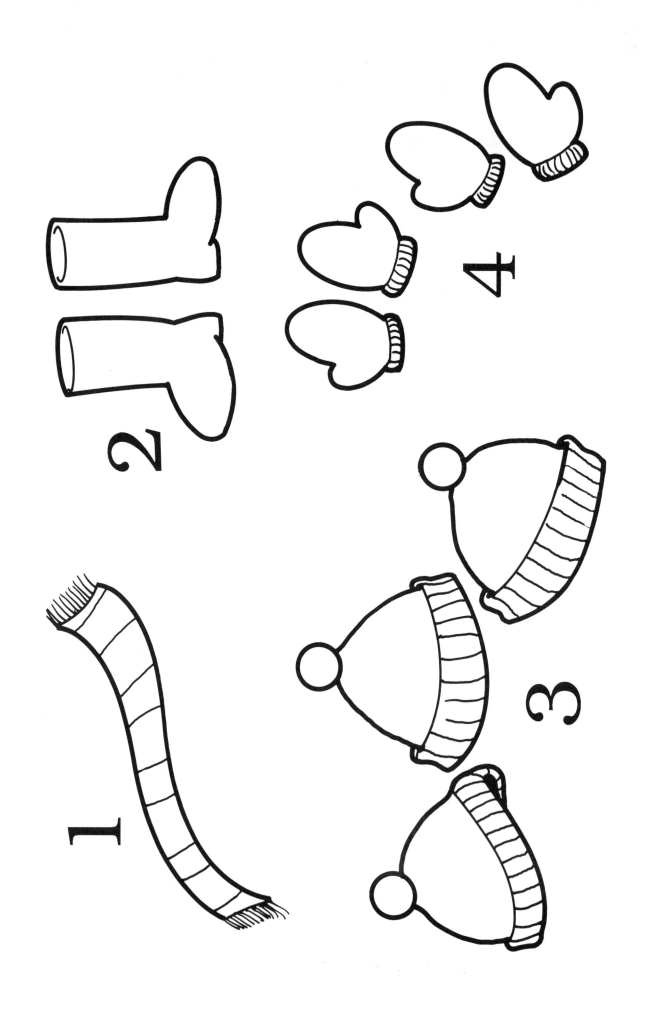

COUNTING CLOTHES

Make: **Counting Sheets**

Prepared Sheets as shown opposite
Wax crayons

1. Prepare a sheet for each child. The items of clothing could vary according to the time of year and the weather.

2. Let each child colour in a sheet and encourage them to count while doing so.

Rhyme: John had great big waterproof boots on;
John had a great big waterproof hat,
John had a great big macintosh -
'And that,' said John, ' is that!'

Activity: Children sit in a circle.
Play pass the 'parcel'.
Either pass a different item of clothing round each time and when the music stops the person who has the clothing has to put it on.
Or - have a large box of clothes in the middle.
Pass something like a sponge ball round and when the music stops the person who has the ball can choose what they like from the box and put it on.

Talk About: Getting dressed - what do we put on first, next, etc.

People who wear special clothes and uniforms.

The theme may be developed further to include:~

my senses
my family
my home
my pets
my toys
my day
my friends